CSU Poetry Series XLVI

Jeff Gundy

Flatlands

For Jack —
well met,
at Wheaton!
Jeff
9/02

Cleveland State University Poetry Center

Acknowledgements

Grateful acknowledgment is made to the following publications:

Ambergris: "A Spectator's Journal," "Competition and Fatigue, or Basketball"

Antioch Review: "All This Talk Just Exasperates the Problem"

Artful Dodge: "The Seal Despair," "The Country as Old Wars and Sunshine," "Seams," "Reckoning"

Broadside (Goshen College): "His Name Was Gerdon and He Ran a Hatchery in Graymont, Illinois"

Cat's Ear: "Toes"

Cincinnati Poetry Review: "Inchworms," "Loon," "An Afternoon in the Country of the Calm Dawn," "Because I Have No Daughters," "And So Heavy with Life the Crust of the World Is Still," "The Best Defense, or Recklessness Part One." The last four were awarded the magazine's prize for the best poems in the Spring 1993 issue.

Exquisite Corpse: "Chicago"

Farmer's Market: "Squirrels," "Tongues"

The Heartlands Today II (Firelands Writing Center): "Where I Grew Up"

The Heartlands Today III: "Making a System"

Hiram Poetry Review: "`The Universe is a Safe Place for Souls'"

The Journal: "For the New York City Poet Who Informed Me That Few People Live This Way," "Ears"

Laurel Review: "Knowing the Father"

Mennonite Life: "Walking Beans," "Chickens," "Worms," "Big Dog and Little Dog, or Where Is God," "The Snakes Inside Your Head," "Morning with Visitor"

Ohio Review: "Kafka in Ohio, or These Sunny Tuesdays," "Fish"

Pikestaff Forum: "Illinois at Christmas"

Re-Visions and Re-Interpretations (Poets' League of Greater Cleveland, 1992): "Worms"

The Rolling Coulter: "On the Day of the Two-Hour Frost and Fog Delay"

Spoon River Poetry Review: "Where I Live," "Where I Grew Up," "Three for April," "For the Soft God Paula," "Crumbs"

Whetstone: "Kingfisher"

I also wish to thank the Ohio Arts Council and Bluffton College for grants and assistance which made work on many of these poems possible.

Copyright © 1995 by Jeff Gundy

Published by the Cleveland State University Poetry Center
1983 E. 24th St., Cleveland OH 44115
ISBN 1-880834-14-6
Library of Congress Catalog Card Number: 95-67572

The Ohio Arts Council helped fund this program with state tax dollars to encourage economic growth, educational excellence and cultural enrichment for all Ohioans.

Contents

Flatlands

Where I Live

For the families of nine other area residents, the day [of the 1965 Palm Sunday tornado] was a most serious tragedy. . . . As was reported then, Mrs. Arnold died later at Bluffton Community Hospital. The others were buried in their homes or thrown into the fields.

Their names remain as the saddest of reminders.

— *The Bluffton News*, April 12, 1990

In my town it's too boring for buggies, except on parade days.
There is however a car with one orange and three blue fenders,
there are men slamming lids on their pickups and turning
toward the kitchen. And the paper lies all over town,
on tables and toilets, the young editor's weird dirge
front and center. Did you think about it? Did you see
the bodies buried in the basements and forgotten,
thrown into the fields like orange peels or mice?

Where I live we are trying to render our losses, but the work
is slow. We say nothing for years and then go loud
and clumsy as the men on state hourly rates who leveled
a mile of thickets for the new bike path. Today, snow fell
at ten on the bright grass and was gone by one.
I don't know how to render much so I keep going,
over sidewalks cracked by frost and thaw until they shift
and rumble as I plod across them, past a little tree
bearing plastic eggs for Jesus, asking who are these people,
what sort of poem are they writing, where do I live.

It's been twenty-five years and the signs
have all rusted. We had almost managed
to forget the bodies thrown into the fields.

We're sorry, we did not know who was
in charge, we wanted only to put splinters
and the smell of broken stone behind us.

We don't know where to find them now, or what
to offer. So we put them into bold print
in the paper, on the front page in a black box,

twenty-five years buried in their homes,
thrown into the fields. We dream them
all over again, flat in the corn

like feed sacks fallen from the truck.
We hear the wind again, tugging us all
toward some laughter, some work to do.

Knowing the Father

It's a good day for sweat to find and coat
my glasses in big smeary salty drops that
I puzzle how to remove without leaving a film
sticky and implacable as the religion
of my childhood, the prayers that demanded
a surrender so ultimate that even as I tried
I could never quite grasp it as possible,
or connect to the way the eggs still had
to be gathered the next day, the yellow
plastic-coated wire basket to be filled
gingerly as I went from coop to coop, shooing
the stupid hens aside, batting at the ones
who'd peck if you didn't slap them away.

I thought I should feel different, the day after,
but if I did it was only in my testing
how it felt, my puzzling: Is this right?
Am I saved? What is it shuffling in
the cobs with me, breathing chicken dirt?
I already knew, somehow: I wanted
a dark, bold sign. I didn't deserve it.
I would have to keep looking.

When the eggs were in the cooler
and supper done I could sometimes
wheedle my father into playing catch.
His glove was dark and old, his fingers
thick from the fields. He threw hard
and left handed. People in town
still talked about how good he'd been,
how he started as a freshman.
Now he was thirty, and that was over.
The ball went back and forth until
we lost it in the dusk, and then
he gathered me under his hard left arm,
and we found the door together.

The Country as Old Wars and Sunshine

> In December [of 1805] war parties moved down the Indian Trail,
> attacking several isolated Wood River settlements on Christmas
> Eve. The guerilla war was on again, and every "Indian summer"
> thereafter, when Kickapoo men had finished their horticultural
> labor, it flared up again.
> — John Mack Faragher, *Sugar Creek: Life on the Illinois Prairie*

Cat runs a squirrel up a tree, dog barks half a block away,
cat scatters. Nobody gets eaten, not today, not here.
And the flat rocks make one sort of essay, the dry leaves
another, the deadfalls. All choices are multiple, some way,
though the sun is gone and the last of Indian summer with it,
the front closing in, dark news of raids on the border,
the beautiful Winslow girl carried off to the cold Sangamon.
We dream her wet face shining, gather powder, salt, lead.

Stop, she pleads. Talk to me. This is not my nightmare,
why must I live it? I whisper back: you have nothing
to repent. You were brought here just to suffer
for me, for old wars and sunshine, geometries of power,
the faint, cool haze of the past. Sleep now. You will go free.
You will remember this as your adventure. Your children
will play in a town whose enemies die young and far away.

Last sun, and dog barks. Cat licks herself. Squirrel is down
the tree, around the back. Nobody here gets eaten today.

Squirrels

Everything leaks. The drains leak, the faucets leak, the shower leaks, the hose to the dishwasher which I spent an hour last night putting a new end on still leaks, and the plywood under the sink is soggy and warping. The house leaks at the foundation where the mice get in, around the chimney where the squirrels get in, and after multiple efforts and pieces of sheet metal I'm still not sure of anything. The roof leaks, not much, just a little around the dormers, and the paint in the boys' room is bubbled and the plaster is soft and crumbly where the water's run in, not much water, just a cup or two here, a few tablespoons there, dribbles and bits. The right front car tire won't hold air or lose it fast enough that I just have to do something, and so every week I try to get to the gas station and pump it up and am always tempted to put forty pounds in it so it'll be longer till the next time, and then I figure it'll just leak faster if it has more pressure so I don't.

I'm halfway convinced that all these things are just what I deserve for my general vagueness and laziness, my habit of drifting off to something else nine-tenths of the way through any particular project. But it's more than that, it's why ocean liners have pumps, why basements do, why this human world is filled with drains and valves and sealants, gunk and foil and visqueen, instruments and mixtures and layers. It's far beyond cliche, these clumsy efforts to keep things sealed against the weary haulings of gravity, the wobbly yearning of the whole breathing world toward chaos and the depths.

The squirrel chewed around my first two patches, once from the inside, once from out. I plant the ladder in the mud and head back up. The wood's barely solid anywhere nearby, but I start bending tin to fit anyway. Even all this talk is only more leakage, mere distraction, the literary world seeping in drop by drop in its sinister way, if I'm not careful instead of nailing this tin I'll find myself quoting Camus or some other dead Frenchman, tipping out over that abyss as I can feel the ladder start to slide in the mud, steady, steady, it leans and leans but it's bound to stop soon if I hold my breath and think light thoughts, steady, if not I can ride it down slowly, surely, the sweat on my palms is a sign I'm ready for anything, slowly I take a step back toward the earth, another, yes.

Making a System

I must create my own system, or be enslaved by another man's.
— William Blake

Recklessness, I thought at first, was the question.
Forget Blake's dream of weaving somehow his own web
out of nothing, far beyond me and everyone older
than four in the hagridden, unevenly privileged land
where I live. Right here in town the newspaper magnate
gets angry once a month, climbs in his Porsche
and drives it north at ninety until it blows up,
not far usually. Right here a tiny dead sparrow
makes a spectacle of itself on the bike path,
its brains eaten out. All right, I know. It's
a hard world, or so I keep hearing, though most folks
could hardly be nicer to me personally. The kids
on my soccer team smile and call me Coach even after
I've yelled wildly at them all through the game.
It's all my stupid male urge for victory, my lust
for the kill, even winning 2-0 bugs me afterwards
and I scheme half the night how to get them to stay put
and to move. Even now I'm drifting into fantasies
of practice drills that turn them wild and fierce
and sure. At least I've learned just talking
doesn't do it.

                    And who am I to claim
that a man can make anything the way he wants it
when last night at 10:30 the old guy across the street
called up. Jeff, he said, what would you think
if you had chest pains? So I took him to the hospital,
leaving his frail wife in her running shoes behind,
and sat with him not knowing what to say until 1:30
when the tests came back uncertain. A long and half-dull
story, yes, me there with an old man I've talked to maybe
twice in seven years, of how I felt sulkily self-righteous
as I sat there missing the news and Saturday Night Live

with Michael Jordan and that first good hour of sleep.
I sat there reassuring him that yes it was all right, that
I didn't mind waiting, that I hoped someday someone
would sit with me. I do, of course, and didn't lie much.
I won't say all he told me. But he and his wife
had no children. They ran a greenhouse, and now they totter
in an old house stacked with papers, letters, testimonies
to his grand work with the garden club. In the morning
he puts on her socks and shoes for her, and she puts on his.

He didn't want to stay. It costs too much, he's spent
too many hospital nights already. But I thought
of helping him in and out of the car, lifting his swollen
feet carefully while he moaned how they hurt. I told
the doctor to tell Kermit that he needed to stay,
and finally he scowled and said All right. And at last
I started to say good night, and then stronger
than I thought he could he grabbed my hand
in his white cold one and thanked me, thanked me
until I was embarrassed, and held my hand, strong, until
they unlocked the bed and rolled him to his room.

Because I Have No Daughters

> When the lights went out they lit candles.
> — Marcia Southwick

When the candles went out the girl
and the boy and the mother hugged
and hunkered, pushing hours ahead
like yellow rafts, so long till midnight,
till daybreak. The dark is not
more dangerous than the light
unless you are a child, a woman
or a man. They knew that. So did we,
but we were far off, and no help anyway.
At last it happened and they met it,
face up, with whatever strength
and beauty they could spare. Don't
get me wrong: It may have been enough.

*   *   *

In the tales of Missapeshu the great lynx,
the spirit of the big lake, he is conquered
only by women. Struck by a paddle,
his tail falls into the canoe,
becoming a great lump of copper.

*   *   *

When getting rid of the father, sweep
your steps clean behind. Leave him
on the island in the middle of the lake.
He's earned worse with his sawtooth blades,
his red meat, his stupid hairy pawing
at your tender openings. Don't say
goodbye, don't wish him peace.
But rowing away from the dim howling
you see the other boat push off

with the she-bear in it, and you smile
and wave and meet on shore. She is bound
for Seattle, you for the deepest woods.
You walk together forty miles, make camp
at the same fire. You have bread and dried fruit,
she finds roots and berries. You compare
scars, strategies for bloodless weaning,
pictures of your redhaired daughters.
In the morning she has made coffee
and pan biscuits. You smile, and eat.
She shows her teeth. This is the life.

*　　　*　　　*

Hamlin Garland said once that there was
"something elemental in being led
by a graceful young woman through
coverts." My wife's at work by now,
answering the phone, saying her name
gracefully over the whir of the copier.

*　　　*　　　*

The coppery tail swamps the canoe,
shining. The women talk as they
turn toward the shore: *What if
there is no more solid ground? If
the beast is not dead? What shall
we feed our boys, and whose daughters
will we give them to?* And at last,
where the land goes under and
the water cracks and pauses,
they hear the breaking whisper:
*The world is not a woman, not
a man, not a child. It is a spider,
a jewel, a thorn in the crown.*

Worms

The worms are out and flat on the sidewalk, most of them motionless but not clearly dead. If the kingdom is upside down, how deep does it go? Far enough to drive out the earthdwellers, the sane quiet ones who need only darkness and dirt? Where is the throne, what sort of subjects are we, how do we defend our borders, or is it that we need to break in? Well it's not just personal, that's for sure. The sidewalks are hard and cold but you can catch your breath and hunker, you can hope.

Sometimes you've got to make a move. Nothing was dirtier than pigs, yet the prodigal boy not only treated his father like a dead man but slept with them, craved the husks they ate. So the father does what, after his buddies have laughed at him for a year? He gives the kid all eight blessings, hugs and kisses and the robe and the ring and the shoes and the good son's fatted calf, thus proving that you might as well go wild, might as well trash everything, God will love you so much when you change your mind.

What are these stories, anyhow? They leave us slack and defenseless, crippled and brain-shocked, dreaming the bones. Samaritan women were treated as menstruants from birth; if one walked through the village, the whole place was in for ritual cleansing. The priests and Levites learned not to touch a dead person, even with their shadows. Can you blame them for passing by? The real story is that love is dirty, like the black grit that fell from the eaves all over me as I tried to nail down the tin that I hoped would keep the squirrels out, just for you. And I had modern plumbing, soap with pumice, and a liberal education.

It's hot or cold everywhere today, lightning blitzed the computer again and the provost says the system is set on random. Ah let's ponder foolishness and slavery, good guys and surprise, tales that bend the categories. Love is expensive in several ways. How many shadows have I noticed lately? They have something to say: it is presence, not absence, that puts us in the dark. Here comes the kid, home from the big adventure, reeking of hog manure and malnutrition, squishing worms with every step. He only wants to be a servant. There's a shadow between us.

Reckoning

Geese flap on the pond, and I yawn
through my coffee jitters the way
we did in the locker room before games,
trying to decide how we felt, how we'd do,
who would shine. No way to know,
I learned soon enough, though afterward
there would be plenty to say. There was
always a surprise, like the cherry tree
my parents nursed along for years.
In the drought summer of '88 it suddenly
weighed itself down with buckets
of the sweetest dark fruit you've ever
dreamed, then died promptly, completely,
as if satisfied.

We've all seen them, the early bloomers,
the ones we survivors admire and remember
as we sit late at table, picking our teeth.
Have you felt lucky today, or gifted,
have you remembered the boy who came
back with a plastic arm, the friend who went
west and then crazy, the girl who drowned?

Oh it's hard to count up, it's easy to judge,
it's too much for mild days in March
with all our enemies distracted by
their own disasters. Time to count,
I say, time to reckon. Somewhere
my old enemies are crying in their beer,
stewing in their miserable juices.
How hot and dry must it get before
they load up and roar off to find me?
It's too warm for March. And the birds
don't seem to notice.

Chickens

for Gerdon Chester Gundy

Grandpa's old blue Ford panel truck turns in the barnyard drive-way, not the one by the house. Dad and I are in back under a big maple tree, setting up the half-barrel we use to barbecue chicken for the big family gatherings. In the general greetings I notice my grandfather's gray shock of hair. I slide over, give him a one-armed hug and a "How's it going?" and shake hands with Uncle Dick. In a thick, red shirt, Grandpa seems heavier but fit. We go back to setting up, feeling the pleasant hunger that knows it will soon be satisfied. I notice that my grandfather hasn't spoken, or met anyone's eyes.

When I wake up, I realize he's been dead for ten years. It's the first time I remember dreaming about him. He was a hatchery man, worked with chickens all his life, moving from small town to small town with his wife and seven children, getting through the Depression somehow. He ended up in a small house in a tiny town, raising chickens and delivering them to farmers a couple of hundred at a time.

Yet he was one of those men that even children somehow know deserve respect, whether they make money or not. He bought ice cream for us, he laughed and made us laugh, and yet he had a quietness with something firm behind it. When we met the last time, when I was back from college, he took my hand in both of his and held it, weighing it, and looked in my eyes for a long moment, as though he was trying to find something in them that neither of us was quite sure was there.

His heart started to go while I was still in high school. Today we would run him through the bypass factory, put him on the walk-more-eat-less program, and he would be good for another ten or twenty years. But then all we could do was watch as his color got worse. Our last game of catch ended with him spitting into the fence, holding a post, not speaking, and me curious and then afraid.

When a barnful of chickens were ready to lay they had to be debeaked, or they would peck each other to shreds. After we drove them into the net, my job was catching them, or passing them along. My father and Grandpa would take each one, slide a forefinger between the beaks to hold the tongue back, and press them up against a boxy contraption with a foot pedal that brought the hot blade down. I can still smell the stink of burning as they nipped the beaks blunt and harmless and sealed off the blood. The chickens would flap and wince as the blade bit in, run away shaking their heads and squawking.

When all but the last few were gone, we wandered back through the empty barn, across the feeders and water lines, across the cobs that had been fresh, red and sweet five months ago but now were an acrid, dingy gray-brown, full of chicken droppings and the smell of too many birds living too close together. We found a stunted one, one the others had pecked at the tail and the nape of the neck until it could only flop helplessly. Did it dream of a space somewhere not filled with its hostile, healthy kin? Grandpa felt the breast and thighs, not looking, then gently snapped the neck, and gently let the body fall into the dusty, broken cobs.

We went inside for iced tea and rolls, tried to snort the dust from our lungs. For days the heavy stuff lingered, after the chickens were caught and caged and shipped off for their fourteen months as layers. They were dumb as gravel, ignorant as flies, cruel to each other as children on the playground. I hated them, their dirt, their scaly feet and scratchy claws, their sudden, stupid panics.

He hatched and tended chickens all his life, and somehow still loved every pullet he vaccinated or debeaked or put to its rest. He loved to eat eggs, he loved to turn chicken on a grill, wearing a glove, holding a spray bottle to cool the coals. Grandma said he raised his arms in the early morning, cried out once, and then was

21

gone. I came home from college for the funeral with a new beard, and stood in the rain with the others of his blood. We ate and talked afterwards, and heard the laughter that emerges when we gather, even to mourn. In the dream the bulk of his belly pressed mine like a claim, like a promise, as I pressed back and held my own.

For the Soft God Paula

1. *Trust Me*

I have been here before, but not today. The geese quack,
water rustles, trees and grasses wave as something hot
and clever floats by, dizzy with balm and joy and a flood
of endorphins. And behind it all, shimmering, the soft god
I call Paula. Today she murmurs, she is happy: yes, she says,
your feints and bluffs are working, though only as long
as you worry about them. And if I do we can begin, can't we?
Or at least pretend that blond light really wafts across
this pond, that the geese in their dim-bulb way clack
and flutter in real time, that the sliver of quartz
on my wrist is counting in the right direction? I can't
tell names or dates but I believe these fragile insects
edging around me would taste awful if I swallowed them.

2. *This Was In 1964*

Why I do I still lean toward toys and games, why does it hurt
so to lose, why do I like feeling sore the next day? *If
I carried . . . If I carried the world . . .* the phrase starts,
but won't resolve. If I fit this place well enough, what
would I learn? This page? There's nothing here about
my running shoes, the caffeine in my system, the near-fight
my wife and I had in bed last night. There's nothing here
about Paula, who is real of course if only in my hazy head,
three parts yearning for the blazing silent wonders
of the world, one part the girl who sat across from me
in seventh grade. We whispered and passed notes that year
in an oddly childish way, considering she had the biggest
breasts in the class and was already getting cornered
by the town kids on hot summer afternoons. Yes she was real,
her smart-ass grin and cheeky swagger, not my best friend
but my friend, someone I could laugh with and not have
to touch, that last year before my hormones kicked in.

3. Or Any Name You Choose

She's elsewhere by now, not dead I don't think, I don't know.
And yes, I have no right to latch my clumsy yearnings onto
some made thing with her name, to make what I can't
     understand
into the feminine. But this is not about rights, it's about
the country that has me surrounded, its currents and murmurs
and wafty breezes, its brush and touch, its flesh and bones
and shivering surfaces. I should know by now, right? If
I carried the world would it comfort me, would it give me
an edge? Would it light me up soft as the last sun lights
the blushing bushes at the shore, the ragged cattail
like a torn cotton swab? It's lucky sometimes not to count
your change, not to play any game but the big one, to dream
only of Paula. Oh you blues, you crows, oh the slight black lace
that thins at the margins of sight, either tearing or healing.

The Snakes Inside Your Head

So Joel and I are heading down the street when he says You know,
Dad, your head has two rooms inside. I say Oh? and What's in
there? and he says, Two snakes looking out. Where'd you see
that, on TV? No! I saw it in a dream one night. Ah, I say. I drop
him off and walk home, puzzling over snakes and what they might
be doing, in my head, looking out.

> One snake sees only bones, hard lines
> and splinters. It moans is this all,
> why not then, might as well. It doesn't cry,
> it builds beautiful machines for opening
> and closing, for breaking things far away.

> The other snake weeps all the time
> for bruises and bumps, for the dead leaves
> soaked and dark, half dirt already.
> It strings long crafty skeins of angst
> and words wherever it can reach.

> And the snakes talk between their rooms,
> they kiss and fondle, argue and agree
> to dream the same dream of the child
> who will save them, who will make
> what is needed, who will love
> what is real and be good at it too.

Next day I ask again, Joel, what about those snakes? Not snakes,
he says, worms, and not looking but just sleeping, just lying there.
Two little worms, and in one room, not two. He laughs easily at
me, so greedy to know, so slow to understand how fast it changes.

Fur

Just as I was leaving after lunch my wife discovered that the sink drains had sprung leaks, as I knew they would when I put in the new sink, and she had to go back to work of course so there I was, with my head stuck under the sink, twisting around in the slimy tangle of oddball plastic pipe and fittings which I pull apart and retighten every few months, cursing bitterly at everything in range, yearning for a neo-classical revival of orderly and obedient forms among the plumbing of small-town Ohio, brooding on the preposterous aspects of the "Whatever is, is right" theory. I try telling myself it's *good* that my sense of competence should be tempered by these reminders, the things I fix that don't stay fixed, the stuff that's more of a mess because of the jerked-over job I did last time, the post-atomic novels with the hordes of city folk swarming out hungry, hardware-laden and value-free into the honest countryside.

I can scare myself plenty just with the black vindictive state I'm thrown into every time I have to deal with plumbing, the way I mutter darkly about my wife and children, heaping abuse they don't need or deserve, feeling the hostile energy crackle like fur around my brain as I twist and push and fumble with tools, swear under my breath or way loud, probe and tighten and test and am only barely appeased if it seems not to leak. I know that I can't trust any of it to hold, any more than I can trust myself to remember what I used to know, how things used to fit together, where I put the tools and the leftover parts against the next time, late, the stores closed and the good citizens in bed, just me and the world of stubborn, dumb matter, the contest underway before I'm ready, the big ugly bruiser stalking toward me slowly, grinning, smacking his fists together, licking his chops.

Morning with Visitor

"Every Angel is terrible."
— Rilke, *Duino Elegies*

And on this day the Lord has made
I want no angels less than holy,
none of Rilke's aesthetic ciphers,

no postmoderns as stylish and empty
as video games. The preacher claims
that the message from the man at the well

is that every place is holy,
that while Joel dumps the Legos
on the hard bench and Ben scrawls

intently with his markers God is here,
among us, as I hush and threaten them,
as I write on the back of the hymnal.

Is some winged creature flapping here
invisibly, hot to change my life?
I prick up my ears, puzzle

what more attention I can pay.
The sermon's nearly over. Ben has drawn
a man with a brown and green face, a cap

with bells on the peaks. *What is it?*
he demands. A clown? An angel?
No — a joker. Do you want it?

27

Fish

1.

It started with dolphins, and with me
astride one in a narrow bay. You
were there too, on another, and when
I understood that the next step was
to eat the dolphins I was nonplussed
but not shocked. This is true, understand,
it happened if only in my sleep, and now
it has been told to you. Did you ever
get grease from your hand on a page
in your notebook, so that your best pen
could barely be coaxed into writing?

2.

At home we have new fish, orange-tailed
fancy guppies whose parents we gave away
a year ago when the tank was crammed,
before they got something and all died
but three. Now our friend is closing down
his tank and my wife went to save them
from the student who has piranhas.
Our friend had only ten or twelve fish
in a twenty gallon tank and they're huge
for guppies, tails like Japanese fans
or peacock spreads but silky, rippling,
full and water-rich enough to drag them down.

3.

Dolphins are warm blooded, air-breathers,
smarter than you or me, not fish at all.
Of course I know that. Did you give up
on me twenty lines ago? While the guppies
are waving their orange flags, spared
and ignorant, my dolphins are floating

happy in some cold ocean, saved
by the shallows of morning, the boat
run hard aground on the night stand,
every hand jumping up at once.

4.

There could be more: eels, elephants, giant rays.
Ah, but, you complain. Are these links
bound into nature? We have more privacy
left than you thought, don't we? More
than we deserve. I could give you the fish
with the blue bitter lust for revenge,
the fish that remembers its life in the egg,
the fish of the 14th of August. They are cold
but quick, not ready for consumption, full
of bright parts I don't pretend to understand.
I'm trying to give them away, all my secrets,
and don't know why there are more every day.

"The Universe Is a Safe Place for Souls"

for Jim Sargent

All right then. So what about Gary Eden, my archenemy all through junior high and the last person I ever fought in the serious physical sense? He was the best athlete in our class, but being a north-of-town Lutheran he got into hot cars and beer and never went out for anything after eighth grade. He wasn't all that vicious, but blond, lean and good-looking in his simple way, and bigger, stronger, faster and dumber than I was.

For years off and on I went around in fear of his picking at me, stealing my basketball when we were shooting around before practice, snapping wet towels at me in the locker room, driving me near and beyond tears long after I thought I was too old for that. Finally once in the locker room he stopped and looked at me oddly and almost seemed to change. He held his hand out. Sorry, he said. Sure you are, I said. No, I mean it, he said. Sure, I said, and looked at his hand. Sure you are. We got dressed. After that we quit fighting. We never talked. We were not friends. I don't know now if he meant it or not.

Illinois at Christmas

Under the winter clouds the earth wanders off flatly in every direction, wide and gray, just slightly buckled here and there, the wavering signs of water and the square human lines marking it. Almost no wind on the ground, but twenty feet up it shoves hard and moist from the south, and when I climb the grain bin to look across the fields, I worry I'll lose my balance. Clumsy with caution I clamber to the top, hold the cross augur, stand up. Everywhere the fields, brownish with cornstalks they don't plow under any more, broken by tufts of trees and buildings, old homesteads deserted and falling back to plain soil as the farms get bigger and bigger.

The fence wire has been rolled up, the posts pulled — corn and beans bring more than pasture, fertilizer's cheaper than alfalfa, so the cattle are crowded onto feedlots, and the fence takes a row that can be planted. The hedges are gone too, and I don't know how the rabbits and pheasants are doing, but Dad has pictures of the foxes that nest in the waterway each spring. Last year my mother saw a deer across the road, miles from any woodlot, looking only a little confused.

Without this land and these people, none of us eat. We have given up something for the bread and corn syrup and tender steaks, but it's hard to say just what. The soil itself, I hear, is washing away, heading toward the ocean and its last rest. We try to convince it to stay. We're not sure it's listening. The bare hills of North China were once a great forest; still, millions of people live there. An old blue-brown pickup putters toward town, paced by the highline poles. I go back to the house for dinner. There is too much here to keep by force, but not too much to lose.

The Best Defense, or Recklessness Part One

Why do I always expect
some calamity? So ginger
I climb, so careful I step,
I pull out my notebook and pen
as slow as the lady who fell
anyway. It isn't right
to be reckless except in short
and careful bursts. The drops
of sweat like rain on the rocks
here, those are natural.
To forget what I have and want
what I don't. To clean out
the pile on my desk except
for the two jobs I've dodged
for months. To consider myself
romantic and spend my days
figuring odds. To watch
the dance of gray water and leaves
and old plastic it's caught
and will hold and to dream
of a language more subtle
and real than the world itself,
salty as sweat, tougher
than plastic, fine grained
as waterbugs too small to see,
hot blooded as this day
in September in the real
Midwest, hearts and engines
pumping everywhere, a new world
cracking the skin of the old
until ha, open sesame,
all the colors go suave and
chilly and brilliant and
fish break the surface, one

two three four five. I wasn't
counting, but now I am. It's
a good day not to die.

A Spectator's Journal

1.

The week the bombing started I found a green pen in the thin snow on the footbridge over Riley Creek. It's a nice one, fine point, no-smear ink, and was full or near to it. Ever since I've been using it all I can, though I'd thought I was settled on pencil for papers (less dogmatic and erasable) and blue or black for all else. But this bright green in a dark winter of war seems necessary or at least expedient, it seems somehow a reminder that all life is not gone, and that all is not well either.

Twice in the last days I have heard eloquent voices speak of the fear and the suffering of Israel, of the children who understand gas masks and the babies who sleep in plastic tents. And this morning a man said he did not believe in Christian pain, Moslem suffering, and Jewish agony, but he spoke the words anyway and left them there with us.

And on this placid afternoon in February the traffic is normal on the freeway near my town, the sun sets obligingly and my children play at home. And the children I should know are already in the dark, maybe sleeping maybe not, and they have no plastic tents and no security systems except for what we said, that we will kill no more than we can't avoid, that we won't kill children on purpose. We are better for that, we say, but how much better I do not know.

The speaker explained that a just war is not the same as a justifiable war, that he would send us articles if we'd give him our names. His fear is real. His grandchildren sleep in plastic tents. We are less evil than they are, he says. I've been sleeping well.

2.

The weather is beautiful and the war goes on. We amaze ourselves. I have work to do anyway, and hesitate before I turn on the radio in the late afternoon. A wet mild winter, and the subsoil is black and damp again. No mines here by the quarry, just an old iron bolt sticking up, sunk into the rock, rusted but strong. I have assignments that mean reading and typing, I have work that means sorting and marking. I worry if a plus or a minus will offend or praise too much, and I am not wrong to worry, even though I am almost sure that lethal implements will play no part in the discussion. There are small flags on every player's uniform and yellow ribbons on every tree and pole, like flowers or fungus. No one is wearing black, here, yet.

I keep feeling there are other rhymes for *free*, that the invisible meaning of the word *support* will suddenly materialize before me. I keep feeling that my blind spot is getting larger, that within it large and clumsy beings are moving through sand.

3.

The last of February and we're walking tall. The generals have lost their wonted caution, and *humiliation* has become our most active noun. We still have few figures and only vague glimpses of the future through the smoke, but the contracts are shaping up and the workers are packing. I've smeared my shoes full of mud that was snow and dirt eight hours ago. The cleats are still nailed up the trunk of the cottonwood at the shore of the quarry, thought no one has climbed them for years. The boys will come home, almost all of ours healthy. Some of theirs lived a month on grass and water, proof we suppose that God loves us plenty.

4.

First spring trip to the nature preserve, a balmy Friday, big dog protecting his lady quietly in the parking lot. He guided me around her without ever quite looking at me, let me go on, no problem. I caught a noise and a glimpse of wet dark fur as I sat down on the bank, muskrat I suppose. The geese honk and blat as usual, their tone insisting they're worried near to distraction, helpless except for the will to complain. I'm caught between the gay loud silence of the world and the trivial sad noises in my head.

I saw the black spider near my foot when it moved, lost it, saw it again. The obvious is not the same as either the ordinary or the sublime. The animal at the shore is lying low, and is it fear or courage if I let it? I could say this is the spot where Gundy changed as little as he could, and that would change it too.

I'm leaving, mildly disappointed that nothing much has happened, when I spot two strange shapes along the fence row. I think at first they are very big geese but no, the color's off and they duck too low when they hear me. They are twelve-year-olds in camouflage gear, their faces painted, embarrassed to be spotted. Their friends are out here, they say, and they're trying to find them.

I wish them luck and drift on, not wanting to give them away. They're just kids. It's a fine day. And I just heard that men love war because it brings them closer to each other, makes them more important than they'll ever be again. Because it is so rich in detail, feeling, and suspense. Only later, if at all, do they learn to love to kill.

Where I Grew Up

> Where the land is flat in all directions, the only relief lies in
> gullies. Where the land is flat, ambush doesn't work. It's hard
> to die young.
>
> — Janet Kauffman

But every section road is blacktopped now
some with stop signs some without
and with the corn high in the heat
you can see exactly nowhere at the corners.
I used to slow down in the summer
and coast through at thirtyfive or forty
only a little afraid of God and the police.

And so I understand about the three guys
from Gridley who started back a mile
to see how fast they could cross route 24
on a slow Friday early in football season
with the town in a television stupor
a twelve pack of empties in the ditch
a Nova that would do ninetyfive
only wandering a little and the corn
ripping past like half a tunnel.

Flat means something to us here.
There are ways to hide the hill folk
haven't dreamed of yet. The ambush worked
like John Wayne's gun and our boys found
their sweet relief and hard gospel
on the sweaty air and nobody
to argue how many rivers to cross.

Where I grew up the good farmers
have filled and seeded the gullies
into green obedient waterways.
Where I grew up we hate people telling us
how bad we've got it, how deprived.

When we leave we find other plains
or plant crooked rows of green beans
and kill every weed we see.

We teach our children all the stories
of the blizzards and tornadoes,
the droughts and the black deep soil,
its grand slow rolls only idiots
and easterners could call flat —
how we love it, how we hate it,
how it did not quite kill us young.

On the Day of the Two-Hour Fog and Frost Delay

By ten the water was back
in its sanctioned places,
the sun was out, the ducks
were circling as they do.

Later I was hiding, unseen
by anyone but God, the water
an empty palm below me,
behind it the sun going down

like a thumb held up to gauge
the size of something, behind that
the distance like the coppery
keen scent of Jesus whispering,

picking up the guitar:
Even my lies were true. Stones
for bread, the nights of dirt
in the face, taking the sword

and dropping it. Fog is
only water trying to believe.
What can save you? Promise not
to talk. I will sing it again.

The Seal Despair

> None may teach it — Any —
> 'Tis the Seal Despair —
>   — Emily Dickinson

I am learning every day. Today
I learned of the Seal Despair.
In the midst of class he appeared before us
and we laughed together as he
honked and limped between the chairs,
ball balanced on his whiskers.
He faced the class with an awkward bow.
Laugh, he said, I don't mind.
I know I'm ridiculous.
We all laughed.

Take this ball, he said. How can I look sharp
with hand-me-downs. Stripes and stars.
It's about as stylish as your mother's
cousin Verna, the one who still wears
catseye glasses and rats her hair.
You can't tell by my looks, but I trained
at the best school there is. I'm an artist.
I don't know what I'm doing here.
I can show you the toss-and-flip, the
roll-and-clap-fins. But you won't like them.
There's no taste left outside New York.
I have to call my agent.
Does anyone have a quarter? My agent
claims she's been talking to Joan Rivers.
I'm glad to be here, really I am. Only
the smell of smoke on motel pillows
makes me crazy, I wake up in the night
shaking and gasping, convinced I've been
taken out with the trash. Have you ever noticed
that a motel air conditioner at three a.m.
sounds just like a garbage truck

as its ram moves to pulp everything
that's ever been made and wasted
into one dripping mass of afterbirth?
Well. And thank you very much.

The students were crossing their legs, doodling
with the floppy laces of their Reeboks.
One in the corner had written it all down.
I stood up and thanked our visitor,
reminded about Wednesday. One asked
if the seal would be on the test.
They stormed toward lunch.
I inquired about his travels
and his plans, forgot what he said.
He left a smelly trail to the door.
I am learning every day, I said.

Loon

1.

Low sun and sprinkles of snow and a huge flight of geese, a hundred anyway, settling on the quarry as I come puffing up. On the rocks just where I thought to sit is a dead bird, a loon I guess, dark except for a whitish neck and orange beak so that for a weird moment I thought it was a bald eagle. But it's just here, uncomplaining, like the fog on my glasses and the big dog barking angrily somewhere behind me. It must have been just passing through if it really is a loon, something else so alien to me that I waste my time brooding stupidly over the mystery of its dead life and of time's arrow which has passed through clean now, head and shaft and feathers.

2.

Community is largely a fiction in the technical sense, I read lately: how many of your townspeople have you eaten with or slept next to, or even wanted to? Nevertheless on this warm Friday my townspeople are out and about, the boys throwing balls around, the old folks in their heavy old cars bound somewhere. I peer through the windows in hopes of a beautiful woman, and am disappointed. Serves me right. Even my dead loon with its hooked beak can only be a cormorant according to Petersen's, although the colors seem not quite to match up. I turned it over with a stick but found no marks or bullet holes, just the odd flattening that comes from lying on rocks for a while, dead.

3.

So as usual it's not far to the limits of my knowledge, or my ability to read the mute, elemental world, so unlike the booklet on coping with nuclear war that we found last night stuck in my father's copy of *Tom Sawyer*. In measured tones we were assured that steps were being taken and moves moved, but that if it all came down those of us not burned crispy would be better off if we stayed in our basements for a couple of weeks, remembering that moldy bread can still be eaten and that sour milk and the water in the toilet tank are safe to drink. Afterwards we could pile up the top few inches of soil, where the particles would be thickest, and then plant our seeds in what was left.

4.

My bird could just as well have died of radiation; it looked healthy, but what do I know about bird health? I know that my young night sweats, long before AIDS, were under the heavy comforters upstairs and the cloud of my faithful and post-nuclear family, as my father and I murmured to each other about the Russians testing the Big One, as I counted the months till spring when they told us the hard rains would wash down. I wondered how to find Jesus by then, and what I would look like, unmarked, quiet on the ground.

5.

By now I know that all my fretting was mere middleclass American indulgence, that the Russians were mainly poisoning animals and other Russians, dumping plutonium into the streams. If I'd been starving in Somalia or shooting up on the streets I would hardly have lain awake so many nights stewing about hypothetical particles in the rain. And now that I'm cooling from my run on a near-dark Monday in November of my fortieth year, stable and healthy and plump, still I find the leisure and mordant resourcefulness to worry far and wide, to wax sentimental for a nameless dead bird as I sit nearby on the shore of a small lake made by hand, as the yellow shine of a streetlight walks toward me on the water.

Crumbs

Two men sat fishing by the shore
where the bank was burning. Two men
were fishing but I went on because
I was running and sweating.
The men were sitting, the bank
was burning, the day was blue and
warm and golden, the waters
freed, the fish hungry, the bank
black and burning.
The corner by the old high-dive
was burning, I should say,
orange slips and darts
still flaming at the back
of the young man sitting on a bucket,
fishing from the rocky ledge,
safe enough from the flames
on the bank and from old man Kohli
who came into the food store
where I was drinking coffee
later that day, when the bank
was burning. He touched
his thick fingers to a slice
of pound cake, took a different one.
He got coffee very slowly,
sat down by the window and ate
and drank, slowly, not looking at me,
chewing his crumbs carefully,
wearing his heavy denim like armor.

It's a daytime half-moon. It's
two boys with a yellow boat over
their heads, walking the shore road.
It's blue water pointing, then
giving up, then refusing to give up.
Keep the line taut. There's

the rock and the water. There's
the black bank, crisp and changed.
It's the life you've always needed,
the tackle, the bucket,
the possible fish. Thin slips
of orange prowl along a border
you almost recognize.
Turn slowly, if you must.

In the Southern City

I was happy to be with my friends on the dark street,
deciding where to have a beer, I knew the night
would be noisy and good. Then a moment's wrench
and I was alone, my jeans wet at the thigh. Time
had passed but I was blank about it so I walked among
the quiet buildings, passed a few people, not too afraid.

I saw a dozen black men, harnessed together, jingling,
singing. I'm just reporting this. They were lashed
together in a coffle but they were not slaves, unless
I had it all wrong they were men who had chosen to gather,
to put the leather on, to pace the dark streets, singing.
They had no whips, no masters but each other.

When they turned in front of me I was there with them
for a moment, somehow I passed through without tangling
in the black leather. They took no notice but went on
and left me, striding along, not too tired, not entirely
afraid. I thought I was heading south, toward the river.
The city seemed vacant as Mars now, and in some ways

I found that comforting. I thought, you know how
to walk. If you keep walking, you will find something
that you know. Something had glittered in the harness,
a buckle or stud. What a story to tell, I thought,
when you get back, when you find your friends,
if they will let you find them.

Chicago

Where do we find good socialist revolutionaries these days outside of North Korea or the MLA? Marx and Freud are slipping badly, Jonathan Edwards all the rage. The photos of bare walls enclosing slag and ashes don't bode well for anarchist radicalism or the benevolent loosening of social structures. The forces of reason loosen their Dockers and slip another movie into the VCR, while outside the streets buzz and rumble or lie silent as Pluto. The experts say that art and sex are merely illusions without futures, but there is some hope for religion. After all these years of believing — in the TVA, the CIO, Howdy Doody, God, the U. N. — this, they assure us, is what we have earned.

Still the world looks its worst through a parent's eyes. Child-rearing changes everyone's body, never mind your soul. It's not enough to look backwards, to see if the hordes are gaining. In Haymarket Square the Black Sox and the Daleys and the pigeons collapse into our joint failure to get anything right. Sandburg and the *Sun-Times* agree: the slums take their revenge. But did we really want a Paris on the lake, a sultry city in the heartland with cafés and berets and dependable clean women among the sowbellies and the futures for sale? It isn't hard to see what we've made: *A separate race, with no place to go and whole long nights to kill.* When the Dogooder Allstars met the gangsters what kind of contest did you expect? Jane Addams lasted into the eighth, shell-shocked but game, while Capone and Bill Thompson circled the bases, laughing. Even a horde of horrified Ohio spinsters couldn't close the bars, and whose side were you on?

When the HUAC came after Nelson Algren he was as ready as anyone. Dante wrote a lot about Hell and never saw the place, he explained; but we've seen Chicago. In the lower circles the hustlers circulate steadily, dodging the bag ladies and the old men clothed in fatigue, piss and schizophrenia. You can get blood from them if you try, but it's a hard sell and a small profit. Whitman stands in a doorway, bleary-eyed, nursing coffee in a foam cup, muttering about incorporating the world. Over Haymarket Square the martyrs to the eight-hour day shimmer in the afternoon heat, and not far to the east the deep miles of water shuffle the cards again and again, trying to bury the man with the axe.

For the New York City Poet Who Informed Me
That Few People Live This Way

1.

We sat in the commons, my eyes scrunched against the smoke.
He hadn't asked me anything. He hadn't made small talk.
He kept reading. Finally he looked up, said he didn't understand.
I tried to explain. It was like being stuck in gravel.

More silence, more smoke. He didn't understand the next one,
either. He started telling me how there are no numbers
in nature, that one and one make two but one apple
and one apple make applesauce, or a nuclear explosion.

He wrote 1, 2, 3, ∞ on the page, paused, wrote 0, -1, $E=MC^2$,
something with Planck's constant in it. He started telling me
about Gödel's proof, but when I said, "Oh, undecideability,"
he sniffed and stopped. He lit another cigarette. I said

I'd be grateful for anything he could say about any of them.
He found the shortest one and said he liked it, it had
an incident and no abrupt transitions or metaphysical mush.
He found the one about small towns and said it was only

about one place, and I should put "small" and "town" in
the title. I didn't argue. What should he care about
fathers in church? Anyway the snack shop was closed,
he couldn't get a Coke, and I felt like it was my fault.

2.

So what are you up to? Dead? Crammed into your study,
writing bitter quatrains about the Peloponnesian Wars?
Drinking beer after beer in some crosstown bar, feeling
like the bullseye in the target? Out here we've been fine,

mostly. My boys are growing, fighting, teaching us all
about power and margins and timing. If I thought
you'd do it I'd say find an atlas, pick a small dot,
rent a car: see if you can get there. If not, stop anyway.

We're out here, working and eating, playing games that
mean nothing, but make us stronger. An old machine
cleans the streets, wakes us to the dawn. We listen.
I remember your name. Nobody else here knows you from Adam.

"All This Talk Just Exasperates the Problem"

You would be too, if it happened. What if
you had no more rights, no more payments,
no more projects in the jar? Alone in the fields
we name our churches, not our houses, which
we cover in vinyl, or fake brick, or clapboards
with half the paint worn off. We have
plywood cutouts of men and dogs, men with dogs,
boys, painted black, smoking, leaning, peeing.

It's the life, or was, back in the old world,
this morning, before we discovered that the stapler
works better with the pointy parts down, before
we found the church in Arcadia with the ladder
leaned on it, a few steps nearer heaven. This is now,
everything changed, the teeter totter broken
in the center, the boys ramping up it and off
into the magnificent ozone. They land squelch

in the mud, laugh at each other, point and laugh.
We've missed the first twenty minutes of the movie,
but know it will come around again as the world does,
the gap so easy to bridge we won't know anything's lost
unless we squint real hard and back up just a little.
No, my eyes are fine, with the glasses anyway.
Well, yes, sometimes they're sore, at night.

Inchworms

It's late afternoon in the upper midwest and I'm hot from the bookstore as a darkhaired young man reads a story he warns us will be long. It's on the news, on the Wheel, on the brow of the girl with dark hair and green shirt who listens intently and beautifully. "Tattered, sexual, and defiant" says the man. His people discuss the World Series and the victimless joke as an empty category. I study the greenery outside. In the cold there's less to worry, these days. There's a dog, a woman, complex interpersonal difficulties related to math and chocolate. If we learn to stop wetting our bed and our pants, why can't we learn the rest?

Did we really want to escape? Do we care if the corners fill with dust and flinders, if the broom will never quite take it all? Oh the flimsy webs in the basement will add up someday, will thicken and gather and make something we can use. The strongest current chemically fortified outfielder hits a line drive home run, and some of us are glad. When the moon goes down we'll watch the stars. We'll dance, we'll smile, we'll tell ourselves things we already know and things we never dreamed, dates, translations, lines of latitude and aberration, phrases and vowels to lead us gentle as lambs or centipedes toward some gorgeous epiphany of cats and dogs and true sexual tenderness.

There is a way, we know, and words to make it plain. A tiny pale green inchworm leans from the lamp, feeling for the way down, then dangles from a thread, trying to get back up. We're talking environments here, rights and suffering, cigarettes, risks, alternatives, what happens to young liberals when their significant others start buying cokes for the homeless at Taco Bell. My consciousness hovers, my conscience rises. The dog kills a kitten, and with tender attention to detail and unobtrusive symbolism we all observe the burial in the backyard. The lovers embrace. Most is forgiven. There are still free refills at Taco Bell. The inchworm tries the other side of the lamp.

Tongues

> And the tongue is a fire. The tongue is an unrighteous world among our members, staining the whole body, setting on fire the wheel of birth, and set on fire by hell.
>
> — James 3:6

A brilliant day in a nasty winter, shorts and t-shirt and I plod off to the woods, to the soggy turf and smeary mud, icy puddles too wide to jump or circle, my feet soaked. Some purplish keen raspberry canes got me too — I'm bleeding on the shin and forearm, pluck a tiny barb and study it.

The pond ice is soggy and rotten, it needs a giant axe or a kid with boots to break it free. The sun's low, the south wind brisk, and four geese honk and settle on the far side of the pond, then three more. I think at first they're swimming but there's no clear water, they just stand around on the ice, call and look, while I hunch and tuck my elbows close.

Do you want the gates to open here, dear friends, the ice to break? I do, I want the flags to flutter, trumpets and oranges and palm leaves waving, I want the little father to circle on his easy wings, calling *come home*. I want the children to come from every quarter, to settle on the soft ice, to stand together there until the moment comes to speak.

If the tongue is a fire, and the water is a frozen tongue, and the flames of hell are pressing upward, how then shall we live? Some day we'll know. Today the tongues of fire snake around the ankles of the world, laughing, licking, and the soggy world laughs back, not yet, not yet.

Walking Beans

1.

To do it right you must slow down, break your stride, refuse to just keep moving. The buttonweeds can fade right into soybeans; only the little points on the leaves and the color, barely more yellow, give them away. "When I find one," my father says, "if I turn and look back, seems there are always two or three more." I try it; he's right.

They aren't bad here, just a scattering, except in the tire tracks where the weed killer doesn't work as well. I say that I wonder why, and Dad laughs, "So do a lot of people." With the chemicals it's better than it used to be. When I was at home the bad patches were more weed than beans; we'd hack and hack for a hundred yards at a stretch, leave the spindly rows of beans poking from the pungent, green wreckage and say, wishfully, "They'll bush out." It was always hot, it seemed, and humid, and no shade even on the ends, and a half-mile round would take most of the morning. We begged and wheedled and tried to avoid it all through July and most of August, but they had to get done.

2.

My mother said to me once, "That was where it started, your poetry, don't you remember?" And I didn't, until she told me again about Kathy and the prickly little weeds we called bull nettles. "Blue metals?" Kathy asked once, forgetting for a minute to whine about the heat, her hoe dug into the earth to sit on. With bean leaves under my cap to keep my head cool I wrote my first song, for Kathy, the little sister I picked on far too much:

> I've got the blue metal blues,
> I'm as blue as I can be.
> I've got the blue metal blues,
> Everybody's picking on me.

3.

Near the road I spot something in the dirt and pick it up. A broken piece of plate, sea-green, fine ridges on the top rim and heavier waves on the underside. I remember then the house and buildings that stood on this forty, where my parents lived the first year of their marriage, just before I was born. I could be walking over the spot where they made love and made me.

The house I barely remember, small and shaded and empty, but the barn we tore down when I was fourteen, and it seemed we spent all summer putting boards across saw horses and banging the rusty nails through. The gray siding and two-by-tens would spring and jump like grasshoppers, and then we'd turn them over and strain out the bent brown iron with crowbars. We got hot, complained, threw nails at the bucket in the grass and missed, piled the boards slowly in the pickup, and finally got to quit and sit in the back of the truck as Dad slowly drove the two miles home. Some of that lumber is in our bookcases now, some still stacked in the barn at home, getting older, gray but still sound, waiting to find a use.

4.

I leave for home, grown up and on my own, bean-walking just a nostalgic interlude. Ten days later I am washing my feet in the tub after a softball game, when I suddenly remember washing them under the tap outside after walking beans, the same splash of cold water sluicing away the fine dust that sifts through sneakers and socks. And then I remember my father washing my feet at church on the night when my friends all somehow got paired up, and I was left over. I must have done his first, because when he finished he stood up and put his hands on my cheeks, hard, and kissed one of them, and whispered in my ear, "God bless you," the only time he ever said anything like that to me.

And So Heavy with Life the Crust of the World Is Still

Sunday after a big rain, the air still heavy,
the creek loaded with silt and fertilizer.
I need to run but my lungs are thick with
too much of some things, not enough of others.
A few mosquitos, lots of sweat, the calm woods
and if I look close the light from the creek
moving on the undersides of the high leaves.
Why should I care about pronouns and referents
when the purple wildflowers I can't name are
standing tall, when the birds are crooning easy,
when the cricket I saw ten minutes ago
is still crossing the road? I thought
crickets hopped but this one was walking,
hustling but not going fast, a slow foot
onto the blacktop and a long way to go,
some distant kin to the little mammal
like a round tube of hurry that scuffed out
fast onto the highway and met neatly
with my left front tire so that I saw it again,
rolling to a stop in my mirror, a week ago
on the way to Goshen. I said nothing
to my wife and kids, and no one noticed.
It seemed to know what it was doing.
I have had it with road kill poems
larded with large noble animals, with
invisible strangers who leave the terrible
bags of evidence to swell and testify,
and yet I know it is not enough merely
to mourn our own small dead, the ones
we do not know or love until we kill them
helplessly, just going where we need to go.

Big Dog and Little Dog, or Where Is God

1.

It's a day for geese to stand
two by two in the shallows,
a day for rest and talk,
a day for mud to start drying.

2.

Don't you wonder sometimes
why anyone would buy your act,
how it is the angels haven't
struck you from the list
as just too flat and unattractive
to keep feeding?

3.

Once I started and stared
upward, then at my hands.
Tiny lines, whorls, hairs
precise and insignificant.
Flex and mysterious obedience,
strength, fatigue. God, I said.

4.

It's a question of looking,
of forgetting the little wounds
and petty complaints. Did you see them?
The winter cardinal, across the street
and into the snowy tree.
The new neighbor's pets, and
my son explaining happily
that the big dog is *younger*
than the little dog.

5.

A man without God
is a stump with no preacher,
a tree with no pillow,
a beggar with no street.

6.

It's deeper meaning. It's between
the lines. It's hidden, like
groundhogs, this is just the messy dirt
and the hole your horse
can break its leg in.

7.

When I touch my key to the lock
in the darkened hall, a delicate,
tiny blue-white spark often flashes,
and each time I am reassured.
No. Reminded.

8.

My mother thought it was a spider
dangling there at the top edge
of things. She brushed at it,
squinted and blinked. No luck.
She drove to the specialist
who told her to get used to it
poised there like a small
black emblem of books and poems
she has not read yet
but will learn to understand.

9.

The big dog is younger than the little dog.
Where is God? In a pebble, maybe,
or a feather, or a wisp of the True Cross.
In a spark that floats
right through your hand.

10.

Yesterday my son told me of the great
blue heron that rose up from the creek
as he was riding out to soccer practice,
how big it was, how close beside him,
how it hung there, five seconds at least,
he said, waving his arms and hunching a little,
trying to say how it felt, so close
to something big and wild and strong
and flying up beside you.

Ears

By August the corn has built its huge temporary space above the quiet fields. No more seeing for miles, or walking any way you please — the rows are tangled, hard and unforgiving, stalks tall as ceilings and hard as bamboo, sharp-edged leaves slicing every free space. Moving through the end rows to chop buttonweeds we push past hard ears in their papery sleeves, collect itchy red scrapes on arms and neck, never see clearly more than two feet ahead, never quite free of some green living touch. I cut a few cornstalks by mistake, but in two days an ear never breaks off.

Fifteen minutes and I'm ready to quit, but since I'm with my father of course I don't. Not that he thinks it's fun, but I've learned from him that in the fields we complain only to be sociable. So we keep going, slip our hooks around the woody stems of buttonweeds thicker than our thumbs, yank back hard until the stems give or the roots pull free. We push the cut ones down through the foliage to wither, stomp on among the sharp stink and the crackle of leaves, flail at clumps of giant foxtail just for variety. We stash the blackest, ripest seed buttons in our pockets to burn later.

Two days at this work, an hour or two at a time, driving the pickup around the section to the worst patches and then wading in, trading hooks around, sharpening them, each time hoping that somehow it'll go quicker, the patch will peter out a few rows in, when we look for the next buttonweed there won't be one. But there always seems to be one more, a bare dark stem among the thicker, knobby cornstalks, five or six feet to the first heart-shaped leaf. Always the heavy, musky smell of buttonweeds in full growth, strong and thick, the smell of years surviving on numbers, stealth and pure dumb vegetable will, of the weedy world holding its own against the fussiest and best-armed farmers in the world. As we head back for iced tea and shade we look out across the fields, say that they look better which they do, and do not speak of what will show up next week, next year, the rest of our years, winters on the bare plain, summers in the corn.

Competition and Fatigue, or Basketball

When I came downstairs the back door was standing open. We always lock it, at least my wife always locks it, but trying to be a good planetary citizen and save a few nickels I've stuffed the jamb so full of weatherstrip and foam that the latch will barely hold. I try to imagine the moment in the night when it let go, what little changes added up to enough.

I walk to faculty meeting on five hours of sleep. It's so cold the snow doesn't even cling to my shoes, the sky clear but pale, the houses closed off, sending only smoke to the sky. A few whiffs of oak among the flavorless gas, some kind of unconscious offering.

I'm sore and almost lightheaded from late-night basketball and the adrenalin that keeps me up for hours afterward. Again we lost, again I missed all my shots, again I yelled at the students trying to referee and was ashamed afterwards. I woke up at six-thirty still buzzing, making strategy for next time, trying to force myself back to sleep.

Yet I feel good, cleansed, as though failing at enough things guarantees some kind of triumph any day. I feel obscurely justified dressed in old sweats and shorts, each claiming a false allegiance, picked up secondhand on my way out of town. I run the court full of the best ideas, waste my breath dashing toward false hopes, keep thinking this time the surprise will be pleasant. I pant and fall down, trying to make miracles, and get up and insist I'm all right, and truly it doesn't hurt until later.

So I walk through cold, through fatigue I'm trying to believe is healthy, dreaming of an energy that will nudge my doors open while I sleep, dreaming of a language that will grasp and fix the shivery joy of walking over crusted snow, of swinging the door shut after a night of trying to heat the world, of leaving my family still warm in bed.

I cross the little creek. After a week of cold only the quickest water is still flowing, making a crooked little track through the ice and snow. The dark water gurgles quietly down a tiny slope, disappears, acting for all the world as if it knows how crazy it is to think of making anything happen, as if it knows that gravity and the shapes of earth are all we need to lean against and flow.

Kafka in Ohio, or These Sunny Tuesdays

Shorts already, records falling,
geese honking and swimming hard,
necks stretched flat and low.
We read that Kafka had almost
no sense of the natural world.

Two fly away, a fat gander preens
and rears and clucks. Don't
be sorry, be careful.

If the father is both dead and cruel,
will the oaks save us? What might
we say, these sunny Tuesdays, how can
we parcel out our yearnings?

> Now I'm the king of the cats, said you.

> Let's go work on our tans, said me.

> I'd better read one more chapter
> just in case, said he.

> You just did it for spite, said she.

> We did it, we know we did,
> we're guilty, punish us, strap
> us down, please please,
> said we all at once.

But let it go. All that's
popped like archaic bubbles.
This is what's real: me and you,
baby, you know it, and
I'm drowning, I'm starving,
I'm helpless and high.
Will you help me, won't you

give me something I can use,
kick-start my carboned heart?

> Four geese loop over the bank,
> settle in the field, squawking.
>
> Eight more follow, then a dozen more.
> They stand in the new wheat together.
>
> A few chase each other, or dig for worms.
> Most look off blankly, in no special direction.
>
> When the father comes their feathers will blow
> free, no matter what they do. And they know.

Toes

Nearly the end of May and I've got this lightbrained feeling all at once, as though while the students are talking to each other I can do anything I want. I'm out on the end of the swing, where the vistas are long and the golden treasures of the world are overwhelming, and so I loll in the sunny sadness, feeling how little I can taste myself let alone pass on to anybody. I sway gently as the ceiling fan turns.

Every day now more students go barefoot, and I watch their feet as they brace and yield to the concrete walks. Those legs curled around the stiff desks, bare toes dusty and contented, make me wiggle my own toes in their shoes, shift my feet, think of the word *register* and the feel of the grate over the floor furnace, warm but almost sharp enough to cut young feet sticking out of flannel pajamas. Warmth and some precious thing close to pain, a clean precarious balance that my toes feel back toward, sure of their footing suddenly as Kerrin's toes in their dainty slippers of dust, toes that cherish the hard floor of the world as I cherish this moment, when it's time to stand up in my shoes, to call the class together, to go on walking.

An Afternoon in the Country of the Calm Dawn

Boom sizzle sizzle boom. It's time
for the end of endings. The end of shame.
What marketing will it take to reach
the ones we want? The origin is scattered
the price is fame. We have learned a lot
about what is toxic, what is base,
let's not lose digits or decimals
or answers straight or gay. It is better
to have a bad reputation, or none at all.
Oh the channels, the corridors, the streets
and houses. Tell the trains about freedom.
Ask the gutters. All the old loss is gone,
undelivered, and the systems plan matrix
waits to unfold itself for us, here. Trust us.
If you trust us what must happen first
will happen, five or six times a year.
What was going in September vanished
somehow, leaving not the finest dust
to sediment your glasses. But we still
have notebooks, operations, a stack
of papers with marks on them. Exercise
your control and it will grow muscles.
Static and noise continue to make meaning
something. The signs on campus didn't
last past noon, even inside. The pink
triangles will not fade in the rain.
Here on the backlot we know how
an absent emblem signifies, we know
the dropout rate is high. The missing
words are not deliberate. Just moving
does not suffice when now is not the time.
But soon, soon we will charge out
of every oblivion and scattered bunker,
we will break for the open and drive
down the field, we will feint and cut

left and pass to the open man, draw
out the defense and leave them sprawling,
slide to the open and find the ball again
on our good right foot, poise and shoot
for the high corner, hard, not caring,
and rise forever toward the falling sky
so blue and clean and full, so near and dry.

For Dale

We were up nineteen to nine, hitting the cover off the ball. The Catholics were shorthanded, with three outfielders and no second baseman, but knowing how they can hit we were still not thinking mercy. Top of the third we batted around, and Dale came up for the second time with two outs and somebody on and singled cleanly, to left center I think. We yelled a little and I was looking around at nothing much when suddenly there was a stir: he was out there in the dirt, lying down.

When I got close he was on his back with dust all over his face, breathing in strange noisy snores with long gaps between. Mark, our left fielder and team doctor, tried to wake him up, told Dale's wife that he had just had a little seizure. She stared and asked the question. I think so, Mark said. A minute later she asked again and he waited longer before he said I think so.

I played second base to Dale's shortstop for three years, irritated him more often than not with my jumpy sarcastic remarks and wild throws. This year I had made up my mind to get along. After the bottom of the second he came in shaking his head at the hard grounder that had gone off his leg: It just went numb, he said. Not that it was hit hard or anything, I said, trying to be sympathetic. No, it wasn't, he said, sounding sincere and a little puzzled. A few minutes later he scored from first and almost caught the guy on second, cruising the bases like nobody else on the team could do.

The rescue squad began to show up, finally, about the time his breathing stopped. Dale lay there in the hard dirt by first base as they slapped and prodded him, breathed into him, finally shocked him again and again and again. Each time the nurse asked Do we have a pulse? Each time we waited but no one said yes.

With a runner on first, two out, and a big hitter up, he'd call over: I'm going to play deep and come to you. I'd nod and pound my glove, wanting to say that of course I'd have the bag covered. Usually the ball got hit somewhere else, just as usually when we got a double-play ball either it would take a bad hop off the heel of his glove or I'd field it cleanly and then throw it hard on two hops into left field.

Finally they carted him off to the hospital. I helped pick up some bags and pads laying around on the infield. A man kept asking about a needle. No one could find it for him. We gathered up the bats and balls, the scorebook, shoes, and children, decided who would take the stuff Dale always took.

I took my kids home, told my wife, went upstairs to wash off, came back down to read books to the kids and then sit in my favorite chair and watch TV. I did all the things I do after softball games, and all the time he was not with me. In most ways, most of the time, he never had been. But that didn't seem to matter this night. I found myself thinking that there is no place on earth to stand except where someone has died.

The church was packed and the weather was beautiful. We remembered him as a family man, a joker, an athlete, one who met the world without expecting too little or demanding too much. Songs were sung and promises claimed, and we went in peace. Outside, I pulled off my tie and saw the sprinkler by the new school, where they are trying to start grass in a dry spring, splashing hard against the wall. Play deep, Dale. I'll come to you.

Kingfisher

for MAS

1.

I need something with a story, she said, something with a center.
This sounds naive, doesn't it? But just as I started in on my own
tales of feeling stumped and disengaged, I almost missed the turn
for the gas station, and that ended that discussion.

2.

I followed her through the museum, nodding sagely. Somewhere
between the fourteenth and sixteenth centuries, she told me, people
learned about perspective, about putting a body inside the clothes,
about halos that don't look like dinner plates. On one wall the
saints looked faintly bored, gazing walleyed into their own shares
of the void. On the next they were touching each other's shoul-
ders, pointing at the child, making a sharp X of attention.

3.

It's all engagement, I meant to say, all point of view. From my
hotel room I looked down into the stadium; my friends could see
the Bowling Hall of Fame, my other friends the Arch. All beauti-
ful enough, in their own ways, clear and fine and firm in the over-
cast evening. The news reported fifteen thousand people loose
that night on the streets, although I would not see them: they were
under bridges, deep in tunnels, trying to hide from the wind, the
snow, and the tourists.

4.

Back home it's the full moon and two mallards on the quarry, a
kingfisher racketing low and hard across the water. Dusk falls
early on Sundays in November, the interstate roars just as steady
and drab as the buzz left over from the Big Bang, which is still
here, now, murmuring below the steady hubbub of the world.

5.

And I'm here too, the center of my little earth, no more no less than the two women talking as they scuff through leaves along the trail. They hear the ducks but move on through their own lives, not knowing that they are here too now, pinned to my page full of lies and appropriations. And I want to rise up, call, entice them to the story:

> *A man went on a journey.*
> *A stranger rode into town.*
> *When the old king fell ill, a great famine*
> *spread over the land.*
> *After years of repose, and without a prince near her,*
> *the sleeping beauty awoke.*

Three for April

1.

The science of clouds is postgraduate but open
admission, and so I have tested the wind,
consulted the thermometer, pondered and come out
without a sweatshirt to sit bemused by the ease

of small things lying in the world, the charity
they offer, and so I am grateful for relations
sparse enough to be elegant, this creek
and scrubby wood and soggy bank

soaking through my sweatpants, none
too beautiful or useful or worth too much money,
so that I can sit and hint about them, sink slowly
toward the body that dreams itself alive.

2.

And the trees stand almost straight
in a quiet I am tempted to call empty.
I refuse to be sorry. I remember birds
I need to look up in the book, seeds
to be selected, bought and buried,
children whose creations will need praise.

But a bird cuts loose from the south,
a sound like a rusty nail being pulled,
and I try to tune and balance

toward a poise like the trees have.
A woodpecker starts drilling. I get up
and start back toward the next thing
to do. Any day now, any day.

3.

Ah, my energy is so low
that putting the date at the top
takes me fifteen minutes,

I sit musing darkly over the states
of my boys' soccer teams and the work
left to do. What words can I

leave out, what tasks abandon
undisastrously? And then
some voice says slowly:

To complain
of the riches of your life
is a sin.

A turtle whaps into the creek.
And stupid, too.

His Name Was Gerdon and He Ran a Hatchery in Graymont, Illinois

He was alone that day, the letter said,
and Sunday after church he stopped
by a cornfield, the sun warm and the wind
stirring up the crisp blank sounds
that rise when stiff leaves meet.
But those are my words. What my grandfather
wrote to my uncle was nothing so literary
and self-conscious. Once my uncle read
the letter to me, and said he'd send a copy.
He hasn't, though he wrote to say he'd tried,
but it was faint, in pencil, hard to copy.

It was my grandfather's last year, and
the death music ran under the words like
a muddy prairie creek. His heart was bad.
He knew. But he stood there, his hands
in the pockets of his baggy pants, and felt
the hand of God was moving in the wind.
You can really feel him there, he said,
on a hot Sunday in the country, with nothing
for miles but you and the corn and the hot earth.
He said it better than I have, though
I can't remember how. I lived
ten miles away, and saw him every week,
but never knew he had such thoughts.

He died in his sleep, in October.
I came home from college with my hair long,
and didn't cry, and went back. And now
I am settled in Ohio and his letter
is still with my uncle in Bakersfield,
too faint and faded to copy well. And so
I put this down, to claim what I can,
to hoard for some cold day to come

my uncle's hoarse voice reading
the shaky pencil on cheap blue-lined paper.
My uncle's name is Gerdon, too.
And out in the country between us
a road lies between fields, a ditch
on either side, and above it moves
something like a music, like a birth.

Seams

1. *Waking in the Wrong Room*

Where land and water meet the water ends,
the land goes under. I feel the tug toward
the depths, tell myself I'm too adult,
and go on yearning. What is real if not
the world inside my head? Remember snake-grass
in the swamps at camp, the way it pulled
apart in sections you could fit together,
the seams invisible and snug?

These planes drone on so capably I've only
seen one crash, and that while I was sleeping.
Only once I had the dream of waking
in the wrong room, and had to lie back down
and tell myself to sleep again, and wake up
right this time. It seemed to work.

2. *On the Border*

We wanted signs and slogans, wonders. What
we have are games. Form a line and find
your self and get it straight and keep it that way.
Every time I tell you to do something
don't until you say Mother may I.
Then do it.

          The creek's been up and partway down;
now it's relaxed again, skimmed with ice
along the south bank. Take a deep breath
and look up to the glow of woods in fall,
nearly ready to abandon all that's left
to do. Little birds and squirrels use
the last light. Sit still, be slow, remember.

Any heat you thought to bring must be
forgotten. Any ice must melt. Any
grief or fretful wonder at the ways
God feeds his flock must not be bartered or
held back. You are an instrument ordained
to settle something. Your heart is strong,
your nerve fair. If your luck holds your children
may grow up safe on the couch, studying
catalogs, moaning for the seas of desire,
ordering anyway.

              If you must worry
something, worry where your deeds are
registered. Worry why you just imagined
the figure a man makes as he shifts
into the gunsight.

              See the red-tailed hawk
that just found dinner in the pond. See
the hill's curve, like a fine rump,
too big and dark for you to hold. Feel
the seam of earth and sky, how every moment
you are on the border. This won't last.
The giants will return, and pity us,
and say we can go with them if we find
our mothers, if we ask them first. And if
we find them, they will say we can.